GOD'S GENERALS

FOR KIDS

WILLIAM BRANHAM

GOD'S GENERALS

FOR KIDS

WILLIAM BRANHAM

BY
ROBERTS LIARDON
& OLLY GOLDENBERG

BL BRIDGE
LOGOS

Newberry, FL 32669

Bridge-Logos
Newberry, Florida 32669 USA

God's Generals For Kids—William Branham
Roberts Liardon & Olly Goldenberg

Copyright ©2015 Roberts Liardon & Olly Goldenberg
Reprint 2020

Second Edition

Printed in the United States of America.

Library of Congress Catalog Card Number: 2015913232

International Standard Book Number 978-1-61036-209-2

Unless otherwise noted, all Scripture is from the King James Version of the Bible.

The photographs used are owned by and taken from the private collection of Roberts Liardon.

Timeline illustrations by David Parfitt.

WILLIAM BRANHAM

CONTENTS

TIMELINE

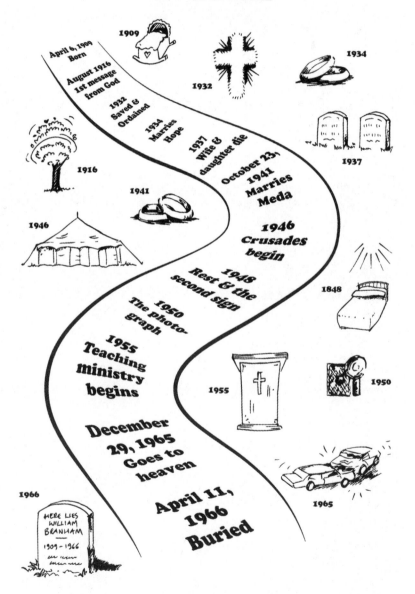

1909

April 6, 1909
Born

August 1916
1st message
from God

1932
Saved &
Ordained

1924
Marries
Hope

1937
Wife &
daughter die

October 23,
1941
Marries
Meda

1946
Crusades
begin

1948
Rest & the
second sign

1950
The photo-
graph

1955
Teaching
ministry
begins

December
29, 1965
Goes to
heaven

April 11,
1966
Buried

1932

1934

1916

1941

1946

1937

1848

1955

1950

1965

1966

HERE LIES
WILLIAM
BRANHAM

1909 - 1966

CHAPTER 1

THE CHOSEN CHILD

The house where William Branham was born

BORN UNDER A LIGHT

God has a plan and you are part of it. Before you were born God knew what part He wanted you to play. Since time began God has always chosen people to do special jobs for Him. It's exciting to know that God wants to use us.

God had a plan for a man called William Branham. As you read his story, notice how God is with William Branham all his life. God helps William and leads him. God is doing the same thing for you, too.

William Marrion Branham was born on April 6, 1906. Now all babies look cute and when his parents looked at him they knew he hit the top of the cute scale. His mom was just fifteen years old. His dad, Charles, was the proudest dad on Earth. "Let's call him William," he announced as he held his baby for the first time.

"Great," his wife replied. "We can call him Billy or Bill as he grows up."

When a baby is born lots of people want to come and visit them. When baby William was born all the neighbors came by. The room was small but lots of people managed to squeeze in.

As they stood there staring at the baby, something strange happened. A white light came into the room. Everyone became quiet. They watched the light as it hovered over Billy. Then it went back out the window.

Some of the adults started to cry. There was something different in the room. The light had changed the atmosphere. They knew that this baby had a special calling from God.

SAVED FROM DEATH

Billy's parents were very poor. His dad had to go off to find work, leaving the family behind for months at a time. It was very hard for Billy's mom, especially now that she had a baby to look after.

That winter a huge storm came. Snow covered the ground. Billy's mom did not have any wood to put on the fire. Every day she had to go outside to find some. It was a lot of work, pulling up young trees out of the frozen ground and chopping them into logs, but it had to be done.

The snow was so thick she could not go far from the house. After several days she had run out of food. It wasn't long before she ran out of energy as well. She was too weak to even go outside, let alone find the wood she needed. She wrapped a blanket around herself and held Billy close to her. They snuggled under the bed clothes together and waited to die.

Meanwhile, a neighbor looked at the Branham house and realized that for the last few days he had not seen any smoke coming out of their chimney. "There must be something wrong with the family," he thought.

He tried to ignore the thought, but it kept nagging him. Finally he decided to go and check on the family. "It's better to check on them and find it's all okay, than not check and regret it later," he thought.

He put on his boots and started the journey across the snow to the house. The house was a fair distance away and it took him a while before he arrived. When he got there, the house was locked from the inside. He knocked, but nobody answered.

There were no footprints in the snow around the house and no sign that anybody had left the house, so the neighbor decided to break in. As he entered, he saw Billy and his mother huddled together too cold to speak, and too hungry to move.

The neighbor rushed outside and got some wood. He started a fire and the small house was soon warm again. He then hurried back to his home. When he got home he grabbed some food from the cupboard and immediately turned around and went back to their house.

Within a couple of days Billy and his mom were back to full health. The neighbor had saved their life.

WHAT IS THAT WIND?

The Branham house did not have any running water. Every day they had to carry water to the house. When Billy was very small he had to help carry the water. By the time he was seven it was his job.

Billy ran home from school one day and saw his dad.

"Dad, please can I go fishing."

"Not until you've got the water, son."

"But dad, all my friends are going."

"I don't care. You have to get the water."

"But, Dad, …"

"No buts, just go!"

That was the end of the conversation. Billy picked up a bucket and started walking to the barn. It didn't seem fair. All the other seven-year-olds got to play. He had to carry the water. They were all having fun fishing while he had to work.

It took him awhile to get the water. It took him even longer to carry it back. A full bucket is very heavy when you are seven! He didn't want to drop it; otherwise he would have to start again. Each time it felt like his arms were being stretched longer.

When he got partway there he sat under a tree to rest for a few minutes. As he sat there, he noticed something strange. There was no wind. The air was completely still. A few minutes before the wind had been blowing quite hard but now it had stopped completely.

The leaves in the tree above him started to rustle. Billy picked up his bucket and walked away from the tree, something strange was happening there. He looked back and saw a whirlwind in the tree. He'd seen whirlwinds before—they were amazing to look at—but this whirlwind was different. It did not leave the tree. There was still no wind in the air, but the leaves of this tree were rustling round and round.

Billy thought it was the strangest thing he had ever seen. As he turned to go home, he heard a voice speaking: "Never drink alcohol. Never smoke. Don't ruin your body in any way. I have a work for you to do when you are older."

The voice came from the tree, but nobody was there. Billy was scared. He dropped the bucket and ran as fast as he could. When he got home his mom saw his face filled with tears and that he was obviously upset. Billy didn't tell her what had happened.

"He must be ill," she thought, so she put him straight to bed.

Billy was so scared by what had happened. He never went near the tree again. Even when he was carrying his heavy bucket of water he would go the long way around to avoid that tree.

He avoided the tree, but he could not forget what had happened there. It was the first time he had heard *that* voice and the first time he had seen the strange wind. It would not be the last time.

CHAPTER 2

WHAT IS THIS CALL?

William Branham as a young man

BILLY LOOKS DIFFERENT

Billy's family was very poor. Even though his dad worked really hard they were still poor.

When Billy went to school he did not have the right clothes to wear. He looked different from the other children and they often laughed at him.

One year a kind, rich lady gave Billy a thick coat to wear. Every morning Billy put the coat on and did it up. When he got to school he would keep it done up all day long. You see, he had a nice coat but he did not own a shirt.

"Why don't you take your coat off, William?" his teacher would ask.

Billy couldn't do it. He knew that everyone would laugh at him. "I'm chilly," he replied.

"Okay, come and sit by the fire then to warm up."

All through the winter Billy had to sit by the fire sweating in his coat.

Eventually he got a shirt. A girl's shirt! It was given to him from his cousin. She didn't need it anymore. The shirt was really a long dress with lots of frilly patterns on it. Billy cut off the bottom part of the dress and went to school.

"That's a girl's shirt, Billy," the other children cried. They all laughed at him.

"No. This is my Indian suit!" Billy replied.

That just made the other children laugh even more. They didn't stop to think that he might be too poor to have a shirt. They were just laughing at him because he was different. Billy ran off crying.

That wasn't the only time the children laughed. He had a pair of pants that only had one leg and shoes where his toes stuck out the end. School was not a happy place for Billy.

BILLY IS STRANGE

Billy didn't only look different. He was different. As the children grew up, some of them started to drink and smoke. Billy's dad made his own alcohol. His dad offered him a drink. Billy loved his dad and wanted to be like him so he took the whiskey.

As he held the bottle in his hands he heard the wind blowing. It sounded just like the wind from the tree. Billy looked around and saw nothing so he picked up the bottle again. This time the sound of the wind blew louder. Billy dropped the bottle and ran.

"You big sissy," his dad called after him.

Billy cried.

When Billy was fifteen he asked a girl out on a date. Billy was shocked when she agreed. He was even more shocked on the date when she took out a cigarette and started smoking.

"Do you want one?" she asked.

"I don't smoke," Billy replied.

"You sissy," the girl said.

Billy couldn't cope with that. It still hurt him when he thought about what his dad had called him. He had to act. "Give it to me," he replied. "I'll show you if I am a sissy or not."

He snatched the cigarette from her. Before he could light the cigarette, the wind sound came again. Billy dropped the cigarette and run away crying. It was clear to everyone that Billy was different. He didn't even go to dances with the other children.

I'M CALLING YOU

Billy grew up knowing that God was calling him, but he did not know God. He knew God had a plan for him, but he knew nothing about God. Nobody had ever talked to him about God.

Billy did not understand why these strange things were happening to him. He decided he had to run away from them. He had to leave home. So when he was nineteen he travelled west to Phoenix, Arizona.

In Phoenix he started work on a ranch. He also learned how to box. He was so good at boxing that he started to win lots of fights. It felt like he had found a reason to live. Now he didn't have to follow God's plan for his life. Finally he was free to do things his way.

At least he thought he was. He still couldn't drink or smoke. He was still different. Billy did not know that God could follow him to Phoenix.

As he sat outside, one of the ranch hands was playing the guitar and singing to Jesus. The man sang about how Jesus had saved him. As he sang, tears rolled down his cheeks. Billy sat and watched the man. Billy could see that this man had something he did not have.

"You'll never really understand this song, Billy, until you know Jesus. Only Jesus can save you," the man said. Billy walked away knowing that something had happened inside him. For the first time in a long time he thought about God.

After several years in Phoenix, God was about to bring him back home.

TRAGEDY STRIKES

The next morning Billy found a note pinned to his door.

"Come to the north pasture, very important."

What could it mean? It was from one of the older men. Billy's heart beat faster.

Why would that man want to speak to him? Had he done something wrong?

Billy raced out into the field.

"I'm sorry, Billy, but I've got bad news for you. We've just got this telegram," the man said.

Billy took the piece of paper and read the note.

"Your brother Edward died last night. Come home at once."

Billy read it again. He had a lump in his throat. He could not feel anything. He knew his brother was a bit sick, but he had not realized he was that sick. It was the first death in their family. Edward and Billy were close as brothers and they were each other's closest friend; they had played together a lot as children. Billy didn't even have a chance to say goodbye.

He packed his bags and set off for home at once. One thought popped into his mind: "Was Edward ready to meet God?"

This question led to another question: "Am I ready to meet God?"

When Billy got home he found out that Edward had asked Jesus into his heart and life before he died. At Edward's funeral Billy heard people praying for the first time.

The minister invited people to come forward and accept Jesus. Billy gripped his seat to stop himself going forward. So many different feelings were going on inside him. He was sad because his brother was gone. He was scared because he knew that he was not ready to meet God. He also knew that God was calling him, but he was not ready to respond.

After the funeral Billy's mom begged him to stay with her. Now that she had lost one son she wanted her eldest son to stay near her.

"I'll only stay if I can find work to do," Billy told her bluntly.

A few days later Billy had a job. God was getting nearer to him. Billy could not run from Him forever. It was time for Bill Branham to grow up.

CHAPTER 3

FINDING JESUS

William Branham

SICK OF RUNNING

Bill was hard at work. It was his job to test gas meters. In one shop the gas was leaking. Bill fixed the leak, but the gas made him sick. He had pain in his stomach and could hardly move. Several weeks passed. Bill was still in pain. The doctors decided something else must be wrong. "We have to take out your appendix," they told Bill.

Bill was not sure. "I've never had pain in my side. Are you sure it's my appendix?" Bill asked.

"We can't do anything else. You have to have this operation."

"I'll only let you do an operation if I can stay awake while you do it."

Bill was scared. He knew he had to have the operation, but he was nervous. He spoke to a church minister and the minister agreed to go with him to the operation.

The operation itself went well. It was afterwards when everything went wrong. The doctors gave Bill some pain killers to stop the pain. As Bill lay on the hospital bed he became very sick. His heart slowed right down. The pain killers were killing him. Bill could barely breathe. As he lay there, his whole life flashed past him.

He had not ever consumed alcohol and he had never smoked, but he knew he was not good enough for God. The hospital room seemed to grow darker as life was pulled out of Bill. He felt like he was going into dark woods. Then he heard the wind blowing.

"This is it. I am going to die," he thought.

As the wind blew more, he felt like he was taken back to the tree where he had sat as a seven-year-old boy. He remembered the voice, "Don't drink alcohol, don't smoke and don't ruin your body."

Then he heard the voice speak, "I called you and you would not go!"

The voice spoke again, "I called you and you would not go!"

A third time the words came clear, "I called you and you would not go!"

"Jesus," Bill replied, "If this is you, let me go back. I will preach for you. I will shout about you from the rooftops."

The vision ended and Bill opened his eyes. His cheeks turned red and he immediately felt well.

Bill's doctor was standing next to the bed. He had expected Bill to die. Now Bill was sitting up. The doctor told those around him, "I don't go to church, but God has visited this man," he said.

Bill still couldn't eat properly. His eyes also shook from side to side. When he wasn't wearing glasses his whole head would wobble as he tried to see clearly.

"We can't help you anymore," the doctors said. "Sorry, but you will be like this for life."

Bill was struggling, but he was alive, and he had made God a promise.

DEAR SIR

Every day Bill read the Bible. He really wanted to meet with God.

Bill went from one church to the next. "Please help me to meet with God." Each church told him he had to do something different. In some churches he had to become a member, in other churches he had to go to certain classes.

In every church he would arrive hoping to meet with God, but he would always leave disappointed.

As Bill thought about it, he could only think of one place where he had seen something of God. When Bill thought about nature he realized that something of God could be seen in the amazing world around him. So Bill set off to the woods to write God a letter.

"Dear Sir, I know you come past here. I want you. Would you come and talk to me sometime? I want to tell you something. Billy Branham."

Bill pinned the letter to a tree and left it.

Back at home he started to wonder. If God was God why would he need to go into the woods to meet him? Couldn't God come to the house?

IN THE SHED

Bill walked down to the end of the garden and went into his shed. When he got inside he knelt down. He was not sure what to do. He'd seen people praying with their hands together so he did the same.

"I don't know what to say," he thought. "I'm sure there's a proper way to do this, but I'll have to do my best."

"Dear Sir, Please come and speak with me for a moment. I want to tell you how bad I am."

Bill stopped and waited for God to answer.

Nothing happened.

He tried again.

"Dear Sir, I don't know how to do this, but I'm sure you'll understand. Can you please help me?"

Bill stopped again, waiting for God to reply.

Nothing happened.

Bill could not hold back anymore. He was desperate to speak to God. Tears started to pour down his face as he cried out: "Sir, if you don't speak to me, I'm going to speak to you anyway. Mr. God, I'm no good. I feel so bad because of all the things I've done. I'm sorry I've not paid you any attention these past few years, but now I want you. Please, come and talk to me."

As he finished speaking, his whole body felt strange. He opened his eyes and lifted his head up. Right in front of him he saw an amber light. It made the shape of a cross. Bill felt scared. God really was speaking to him.

Bill heard a voice, but he did not understand what it said, then the cross disappeared. Bill was shocked.

"Sir, I didn't understand what you said, but I guess you're telling me all the bad stuff I've done is on that cross. Could you please speak to me again? If you speak English that would be great, but if not I understand."

As he finished speaking, the cross appeared again. As he closed his eyes, he felt free. For the first time in his life he felt real peace. When he opened his eyes the light had gone.

Bill rushed into the house with a huge smile on his face. He knew he had met with God and he would never be the same again.

A few nights later his mom spoke to him. "Bill, I had a dream about you last night. I dreamt you were preaching to the whole world."

Bill was shocked. His mom never had dreams. God was still speaking to him, not just through the signs around him but through his mother. He wanted to obey God, so he started to preach.

CHAPTER 4

SERVING JESUS

Baptizing converts

PREACHING THE WORD

Bill was out on the street preaching about Jesus when a man came up to him.

"I used to be a priest. You don't believe all that nonsense in the Bible do you?"

"I certainly do!" Bill smiled.

"That Bible is a dangerous book. It should be banned."

"This is a free country—you're welcome to believe what you want to. I believe the Bible is true," Bill replied.

"So you really believe that God exists. You believe that Jesus died and came alive again!"

Bill just stood there, he had not been a Christian for very long, but he knew that some people were not kind to Christians.

"Tell me, young man, what are the five senses?"

Bill replied, "Hearing, seeing, smelling, taste, and touch."

"Good, now tell me, young preacher, have you ever seen God?"

"Yes, I saw him in a vision last week ...." From the moment Bill was saved in the shed he often saw visions from God.

"No, not in a vision. I mean with your eyes." Bill did not reply.

The man continued, "Have you ever felt God?"

"Yes, I feel Him all the time in my heart."

"Then bring Him here so I can feel Him in my heart too!"

"Sir, you need to believe in Jesus by faith before you can feel Him."

But the man did not believe. He knew he had made his point; you cannot touch God like you touch a chair.

Bill prayed quietly. Then God gave him an idea.

"Sir, you seem like a very bright man. It seems like you have a clever mind. Can I ask you a question?"

"I sure do have a good mind. My mother didn't make me a fool. Go ahead and ask," the man replied.

"Has anyone ever seen your mind?"

"Scientists can cut open my head and see my brain," the man replied.

"I'm not talking about your brain. I'm talking about your mind—they are two different things." Bill carried on, "Has anyone ever touched your mind, tasted, heard or smelt your mind?"

The man did not know what to say. He blurted out, "But I know I've got a mind."

"And I know I've got a God, too."

Bill then took a pin and jabbed the man.

"Ow! What are you doing?" the man yelled.

"Did you feel that?" Bill asked.

"Of course I did," the man replied.

"That's funny because I didn't feel anything."

"Let me stick you with the pin then you will feel it all right," the man snarled.

"That's exactly my point. If you will accept Jesus like I did you will feel Him like I do."

Bill had won the argument. Of course people don't get saved when you win arguments, they just go away annoyed. Bill knew that God had to reveal himself to people for them to know Him. God had given Bill the words to say so that he could answer this man who did not believe in God.

FINDING HOPE

Bill was busy at work when he saw a beautiful lady walk by.

"Hello, Ma'am," Bill said. "My name is Billy Branham."

"Hello, Billy," the lady replied, "my name is Hope."

Bill kept talking to her, asking more questions. There was something special about this lady. He wanted to see her again.

"Do you know God, Ma'am?"

"I'm a Christian and I go to the local Baptist church."

Bill was so happy. Now he knew how he could see her. "I've just become a Christian too! I'm not really going to any church yet. Maybe I'll come to your church."

Hope smiled, "I'll save you a seat."

That Sunday he slipped into the church. It was quite full, but true to her word, Hope had saved him a seat. That was a start of a very special friendship. In a couple of years' time they would be married.

GET OUT THERE AND PREACH

Other people started to notice Bill. It was clear that God wanted him to preach. So they let him. Bill was ordained as a minister when he was twenty-three years old. He preached in whatever building he could find.

In June, 1933, Bill got hold of a large tent and started preaching. Three thousand people came out to hear him. Bill was only twenty-four years old, but already he had a bigger crowd than many people who were twice as old as him. By the end of the meetings 130 people were baptized.

Bill took them all down to a river to baptize them in water. As he was baptizing them in the water, he heard the sound of the wind again. A light appeared above him. Then he heard a voice speaking.

Hundreds of people were watching the baptism. Lots of them saw the light. Some even heard the voice. Some people started to worship God; others were so scared that they ran away.

Bill simply stood there, shocked, as the voice spoke: "You have a message that will help get people ready for Jesus to come back."

Some people thought that Bill was "the" person who would come before Jesus. The voice only described him as "a" person. Even so, it was clear that God had a special plan for Bill's life.

CHAPTER 5

HOLY ROLLERS

William Branham preaching

WHO ARE THESE PEOPLE?

Bill had gone fishing. He loved to fish and he loved to hunt. It gave him time to think. It gave him time to enjoy being in God's creation. On his way home he saw a huge crowd of people going to a meeting in a tent. Immediately he was interested. Who could all these people be going to see? Bill decided to go to the meeting.

As he walked in, people were singing and clapping. It was much livelier than meetings in his church. The preacher talked about the baptism of the Spirit and Bill was immediately interested. That night he sat with the other ministers and each person was asked to stand up and introduce themselves.

"I am Evangelist William Branham," Bill stated. He then sat back down again.

The preacher that night was an elderly man. He walked slowly to the pulpit. Bill looked at him and felt sorry for him. "The poor man doesn't even have the energy to stand for a long time. How is he going to preach?"

But Bill was wrong. As the man spoke, he seemed to open up Heaven. His words shot through the crowd as he spoke of the God who was before the world existed telling of God's work right through the time when Jesus will come back to the Earth. By the time the old preacher had finished he was full of energy and jumping around like a young man.

Bill looked at the preacher. He no longer felt sorry for the man; instead he felt sorry for himself. This man had something that he didn't' have and Bill wanted it!

NOW IT'S YOUR TURN

Bill could only go to the meetings for one more day. He had been sleeping in a field and he had no money left to eat. On that last day he turned up in his scruffiest trousers and sat with the crowd.

The leader of the meeting stood up.

"We've just had our youngest minister lead the testimony time. Now the second youngest minister is going to preach: Reverend William Branham, please come forward."

Bill did not move. "I can't preach to these people. I've not got anything ready for them. They are all amazing preachers. What could I say? I'm not even wearing decent clothes." He sat there looking down.

"Does anyone know Reverend William Branham? Is he still here?"

Bill felt the person next to him nudge him in the ribs.

"Do you know who this Branham person is?" the man asked him.

Bill could not lie, "Yes, I do."

"Well go and get him then."

"I am him. But I can't preach. Look at what I'm wearing to start with. I've not even got a suit on!"

"Listen, these people don't care what you look like. They want to hear what's on your heart."

Bill squirmed in his seat. "Please don't tell anyone."

But the man ignored Bill. He stood to his feet and shouted: "He's here. William Branham is here!"

Bill could not run away. He had to go forward.

As he walked to the platform, he saw the microphones. He had never used them before. He was so nervous. Bill prayed desperately: "God, you've got to help me now."

A NEW SERMON

Bill opened his Bible and a verse caught his eye: "The rich man opened up his eyes in hell."

He started to preach. "This man had no Christians to help him. There was no church, no flowers, and no God."

As Bill preached, his style was different from the usual preachers. Normally he would stand still behind the pulpit and preach a very formal sermon.

Now he was preaching from his heart. His emotions were shining through and God was taking hold of him. The whole crowd knew that God was speaking through him. The man next to him had been right. They didn't care what he looked like on the outside, they just wanted to hear what was in his heart.

After the service a man came up to Bill.

"I've got a church in Texas. Will you come and hold a couple of weeks of meetings there?" Bill was amazed.

"Sure," he said and he wrote down the man's name and number.

Another man came, "I've got a church in Florida. Could you hold some meetings for me too?"

"Okay," and Bill wrote down the man's name and number.

More people kept coming up to him until he had so many invitations that he would be busy all year speaking. God was clearly up to something.

Bill jumped into his car and drove home as the happiest man alive. He knew that he had met people who really knew God. This was where he wanted to be. This was what God was calling him to do.

He couldn't wait to tell his wife.

NO!

As Bill ran into the home, his wife looked at him.

"What's up with you?" she asked. "You look so happy."

"I am. I've met the happiest people I've ever seen and they love Jesus. They are Pentecostals. I'm different since I've been with them. Now I've been invited to preach all over the country."

Bill paused.

"Will you go with me, Hope?"

Hope did not wait to answer, "Of course I will. I promised God that I would follow you wherever you go for the whole of my life."

Bill ran to tell his mother, "I'm going to be leaving soon to travel, mom."

"What will you do for money?"

"God will look after us," Bill replied.

She looked at Bill carefully. She could see he was different. "You know son, we used to have this kind of religion in our church. I know it is from God. God bless you as you go."

But not everyone agreed.

"God has given you this church here. You need to stay and look after it," some said.

"You won't be able to feed your family if you go. Your wife will eat one day and starve the next."

Hope's mother was definitely against it. "Don't you know that's a bunch of holy rollers? Do you think you're going to drag my daughter around people like that...? Don't be so ridiculous! That's nothing but trash that the other churches have thrown out."

Bill listened to her. He called each of the people on his list and told them he would not be coming.

For the rest of his life he regretted that decision. He knew God was calling him and he did not go. He had been worried that life would be too hard if he went. But it would not have been harder than what was about to happen to him in just eight months' time.

CHAPTER 6

WHERE IS HOPE?

William and Hope Branham

FLOODED WITH PROBLEMS

Eight months after Bill had decided not to go and preach, trouble came to town.

In January, 1937, it started to rain across the Eastern part of America. A lot of the rain that fell poured into the Ohio River and the river began to rise. There was so much water that it could not stay in the river; the whole area started to flood. It was the worst flood ever recorded even up to this day. 100,000 people became homeless as the water flooded their home.

Bill was right in the middle of it. Hope was at home suffering from a lung infection. Bill knew it was his job to look after her. At night he would go on duty, marching up and down the river to check that it was still within its banks. The people were saying that soon it would flood in Jeffersonville, Indiana.

One night it did. As Bill was walking along the river banks, he heard a whistle. The river had broken through the flood wall. In fact it came nearly 6 meters above flood level!

Fire engines started to move and then everyone in the town woke up. People had to leave the town at once or risk being caught in the flood. Bill rushed back to be with Hope. She could not leave town because she was too sick, but the government had set up a hospital on higher ground. Bill took her and the children through the storm to the temporary hospital.

On the way the children suffered from the cold rain. At the hospital they were too sick to leave. The staff was overworked in the hospital and because the hospital had only just been set up, there were not enough beds for the people. But there were more people suffering in town. Bill wanted to stay but he knew he had to go and help others to escape.

SHE IS SAFE

Bill got in a boat and went down the river to see who needed help. As he went down the river, he heard a lady crying for help out of a window. The lady and her children were trapped in the house. They had no way to escape the water. Bill had arrived just in time. He helped the family into the boat and took them to higher ground. Their home was destroyed, but at least they were safe.

Bill returned to look for more people. The river was flowing faster and faster. There was so much water that Bill could not control the boat anymore. He had been driving boats for many years but he had never faced waters like this. The waters were pushing his boat all over the place.

Bill was not sure he would get out alive. He battled through the water and finally made it back to the hospital to see Hope. Bill had been gone for four hours. In that time the water had reached the hospital and as he went inside, he realized that it was empty.

Bill started to ask around. Nobody knew where Hope was. She had been taken from the hospital but nobody could tell him where she had gone. For hours he ran around trying to find answers. Finally one official told him, "They were all taken on a train to Charleston. It's about twelve miles from here."

Bill rushed to the train track to see if he could get to her. But the water had flooded the track. Now he did not know if she had made it safely or if the train had been washed away in the flood.

Each time he thought she was safe more bad news seemed to come. For a long time he heard nothing. Then the news came: "The train made it through. Your wife is safe."

Bill was ecstatic. He jumped into a speed boat and started to drive through the water, but he had forgotten how strong the water was. As his boat was whipped around by the strong currents, it got washed up and stuck on a small island and could not be moved. A few other people were stuck on the same bit of land. They did not have much food and Bill still did not know for sure what had happened to his family.

For two weeks he was stuck. Two weeks of not knowing. As soon as he could, though, he carried on his search for his wife.

MEETING AGAIN

When he found out she was in Columbus he went to the nearest train station.

"Sorry, mate, there have been loads of floods in the last few weeks. The trains aren't working."

Bill felt lost. What could he do? A friend drove past. "Bill, I've found a secret way through to Columbus. It avoids the water. Get in and let's go get your family."

Bill jumped in the car. His heart was pounding with excitement and fear. He was excited to be going to his family but afraid of what he might find when he got there.

They stopped at a Baptist Church. The building had been turned into a hospital to help the sick. Bill rushed in and frantically started calling and searching for Hope until he found her. She was very sick, but at least she was alive. Bill held her thin hand as she opened her eyes to look at him. She spoke quietly. "It's good to see you, Bill. The children are with my mom. They are both sick too."

Dr. Adair knew she was very sick. He was Bill's friend and he wanted to help.

"Go home, Bill, and get things sorted out. Then you can take Hope home to be with you. She has TB in her lungs and it's not getting better."

Bill cleaned the house up after the flood and tried to make things ready for his family.

IT'S NOT GOOD NEWS

Back at home Bill worked hard to earn money. It had cost him a lot to pay for all the treatment in the hospital and now he was in debt. No treatment was making her better. One day he got a call.

"If you want to see your wife alive, you need to come now."

Bill dropped everything and rushed to the hospital. As he walked in, he met his friend Dr. Adair. Bill did not need to ask; he knew he got there too late.

"Dr. Adair, please come in with me to see her one last time."

Dr. Adair shook his head. "I can't do it, Bill. She was like my sister. I can't see her like this."

Bill walked into the room. A sheet had been pulled over her face. Bill pulled it back to look at his wife. Her body was pale and without life. He held her up in his arms and sobbed. "God, please... let me speak to her one more time." For weeks he had prayed for God to spare her, now the end had come. "Honey! Answer me."

A bit of life returned to Hope and she lifted up her hands to Bill. She was too weak to talk, she could only whisper. Bill leaned close to her mouth to listen.

"I was nearly home, Bill. Why did you call me back? Heaven is beautiful, Bill. You've preached about it, but it's even more amazing than you said. Please marry someone else when I've gone. I don't want you to be alone, Bill. Someone who will look after the children."

"Darling, don't talk like that," Bill was crying.

"I don't mind going now that I've seen Heaven. Bill, will you promise me one thing—keep preaching this wonderful gospel. God is going to use you."

She pulled Bill closer and kissed him goodbye, then she drifted back into the paradise of Heaven.

CAN IT GET ANY WORSE?

That night Bill lay on his bed thinking about his family. How would his children cope without their mom? A knock on the door startled him.

"Bill, your baby girl is dying. I am so sorry."

When Bill saw his baby she was in pain and suffering from TB like her mother, but this time the infection had gone to her brain. Her tiny body was twisting up as the disease took over her brain.

"God, please don't take my baby too. Please heal her," he cried.

God did not answer this prayer. Bill saw a vision of a black cloth coming over his baby. Right then he knew that she was going to die. Two days later she was buried in her mother's arms. Sadly, Bill thought that God was punishing him. He had not gone to preach in the Pentecostal churches. God had told him to go, but he had stayed to keep his family safe. Now his family was destroyed.

The safest place to be is right in the middle of God's plan for your life. God wants people who will obey Him. God used this horrible situation to help Bill. Whenever Bill saw people suffering he knew what it was like to suffer. Because of this double tragedy in his own family he saw life differently. Now he could cry with other people when they were hurting.

We don't always understand God's ways. If we did, we would be as great as God is. Sometimes all we can do when things go wrong around us is to decide to keep trusting God anyway. Bill did not reject God because of this. Instead, he chose to get closer to God. After this season of mourning and healing, William Branham was now ready to step into the main calling for his life.

CHAPTER 7

VISIONS OF THE FUTURE

Branham Tabernacle, the church which William Branham led

BE MARRIED

After Hope and baby Sharon had gone to Heaven, Bill was left taking care of his son. He continued to work and to lead a church called Branham Tabernacle. At times he felt so sad that he did not think he could carry on.

But God had not given up on him. Bit by bit Bill's life was coming back to normal. He was really helped by his housekeeper, Meda. She was a wonderful lady who would do anything to help the family. That's why Bill was shocked when God told him to marry her. He had never thought about it. As he lay on his bed in the boat he lived in, he thought about her.

She had looked after his son, Billy Paul, for five years. Now Billy Paul was six years old and he really needed a mother. She was a good woman and God's voice had spoken very clearly to him:

"Go and marry Meda on October 23rd of this year."

It was the same voice that Bill had learned to obey in the visions that he saw. So on October 23, 1941, nearly five years after Hope had died, Bill married Meda.

God had shown Bill what to do, Meda had agreed and Bill had obeyed.

IT'S HAPPENING ALL AROUND ME

Bill had been seeing visions often in his life. Recently a lot of the things he had seen started to happen. Back in 1933, he had seen a vision of Mussolini invading Ethiopia. This happened in 1935.

At the same time he had seen a vision of a young man called Adolf Hitler from Germany starting a second World War. At the time nobody thought this would happen. Who would want to go back to war so soon? They could all remember the horrors of the First World War that ended in 1918.

In 1939, the Second World War was started by Adolf Hitler.

In the same vision he had seen that Franklin Roosevelt, the President of the United States of America, would be elected for a fourth term. No president had done this before and Roosevelt had only just become the president at the time. In 1944, Roosevelt won his fourth election in a row.

Now in 1945, as the Second World War came to an end, Bill started to see visions more often.

BE HEALED

One night Bill was at his mom's house for the night. As he lay on the bed in the spare room, he suddenly found himself outside. "That's strange," he thought, "I've not moved but here I am outside. It must be another vision."

In the vision he walked into a house that was in front of him. In that house lay a boy with legs that were badly crippled. Bill heard the familiar voice of the visions, "Can this child be healed?"

"Sir, I don't know," Bill answered.

"Ask the father to bring the boy to you. Pray for him and he will live."

He saw the father carrying the boy. As he prayed for the boy, the father dropped him. The boy landed on his left leg which immediately untwisted and became normal. Then the boy stepped onto his right leg. He took three steps and was totally healed.

A milk moustache covered the boy's top lip as he spoke, "Brother Bill, I am perfectly whole."

Bill was taken to another vision. In this place he was shown directions to a house. When he got to the house he saw a sign saying, "God Bless This Home." Inside the home a teenager lay in bed. Both her legs were all twisted up by a disease called polio. One arm had also shriveled up. It was totally useless.

The voice inside Bill's spirit said, "Put your hands on her stomach and pray."

Bill walked over and did as he was told. The girl cried out, "Praise the Lord!" Her arm filled out and her legs untwisted. She was totally healed.

"Brother Branham! Brother Branham"

Someone was calling him. Bill found he was back in his mother's house. He was confused about what had happened. It must have been a vision, but now a real voice was calling him.

JUST LIKE HE SAW IT

A man stood at the door. "Brother Branham. Please, can you pray for my little boy? He is very sick." As Bill got ready to pray, he recognized one of the men who was riding with them. The man had been in the vision he had just seen.

"Sir, your boy is about three years old. He is wearing blue trousers, isn't he?"

"Yes."

"Your house has a white door and two rooms inside. One is ...."

"Brother Bill, have you ever been to my house?"

"I've only just left there."

The man was confused.

"God gave me a vision of your home. Your son is going to be healed.

When Bill got to the house the boy was close to death. He had pneumonia. His lungs were full of infection. He could not breathe. In the vision the boy could not walk because his legs were crippled. Now Bill stood by the bed. He could see that the boy could not walk because he could hardly breathe.

Bill prayed for the boy, but instead of getting better he got worse.

Looking around the room, Bill noticed that an old lady he had seen in the vision was not there.

He waited and waited but the lady did not come.

"I've got to go now," one man said. Bill didn't understand. That man had been in the vision. If the man left, then even if the lady came, the vision would not be complete.

The man put his coat on and was about to leave when there was a knock at the door.

An old lady stood there. It was the same lady from the vision.

As Bill watched, each person stood in the exact position that he had seen them in the vision.

He prayed for the boy and immediately the boy looked better. Bill remembered how the boy had taken three steps in the vision. At that moment he realized that each of those steps was one day. "He will be totally healed in three days' time," Bill announced.

When Bill visited a couple of days later, the boy came up to him. He had been drinking milk and so had a milk mustache. "Brother Bill," he said, "I am perfectly whole."

Everything had happened just as Bill had seen it.

That Sunday Bill told the church what had happened. He also told them about the second part of the vision.

"This afternoon I'm going to go to that house and God is going to heal that girl," he told them.

Some members of the church went with him. They wanted to see God heal. On the way Bill told them all the details of the vision. He told them how they would meet a man who would show them directions. He told them the clothes the man would be wearing. He told them what the house would look like. He told them what the girl's room looked like. He described the girl and how sick she was and then he told them how she would be healed.

It all happened just as he had seen it. When one of the ladies walked into the girl's room she saw it was just as Bill had described it. She was so amazed that she fainted!

The girl with a shriveled arm and two crippled legs was healed immediately. Just one thing was bothering Bill:

where did these visions come from? Was it God or the devil? He had asked some ministers and they had told him God did not speak through visions anymore. Were they right?

He was getting more and more visions. Each one was coming true, but that did not mean they were from God. Bill decided to go by himself and seek God. He needed to know what was happening. He had no idea that something was about to happen that would change his life forever.

CHAPTER 8

TWO SIGNS

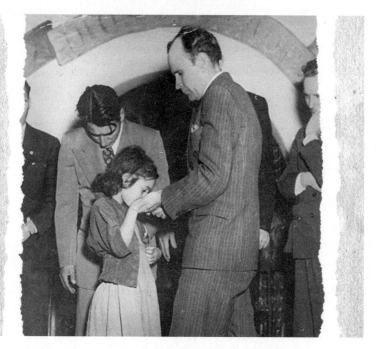

Praying for a sick girl who was healed

LORD, SPEAK TO ME

Bill had his Bible open and was calling out to God. He had gone to a cave where he could hide away from people and seek God. It was Tuesday, May 7, 1946.

"Please Lord; I just want to follow you with all my heart. I am sorry that I have not always done what you asked me to."

He prayed through the day and into the evening. At around 11 o'clock he sat up. He noticed a flashlight by the entrance of the cave. He was surprised as he did not think anyone would be coming past this way, especially so late at night.

He looked out, but could not see anyone. When he looked back at the light it started to spread out across the room. It was like a star was in the cave. Bill could not take his eyes off it. He heard footsteps walking across the room. Then out of the star he saw the feet of a man. As Bill continued watching, a man stepped out of the light.

The man was no ordinary man. He was twice as big as any human. He wore a white robe and had black hair. Bill was scared. He could not believe what he was seeing. The man looked right at him and saw he was afraid.

The man spoke, "Don't be afraid."

Bill knew the voice. It was the same voice that had spoken to him from the tree when he was seven years old. It was the same voice that had told him not to smoke, drink, or ruin his body. Now Bill was meeting the person behind the voice.

"Almighty God has sent me to you. Not many people understand your life. The strange things that have happened to you are to show you that you have been chosen to take the gift of God's healing into the world."

God had sent an angel with a message for him. Bill was listening. He knew that angels had sometimes been sent to the apostles to speak messages; he knew this was in the Bible. Now he was ready for this message from God.

The angel carried on. "If you will really mean what you say and can get people to believe you, then nothing will be able to stand against your prayers, not even cancer."

THE FIRST SIGN

Bill didn't feel ready for this job. He had not spent long in school. He did not feel ready. Why would anyone listen to him?

Many of the people in the Bible felt the same way when God called them. Just look at Moses and Gideon from the Old Testament. Read about Ananias who prayed for Saul to see again. These people knew that they could not do what God was asking them to do on their own.

The angel continued speaking.

"Moses was given two signs so that people would believe God had sent him. God will also give you two signs."

The angel described the first sign.

"If you are praying for somebody, hold their right hand with your left hand. Then just stand quietly. As you stand there, you will be aware of something happening inside you. When you pray, if your body goes back to normal, then you know that person has been healed. If it does not, just pray for that person to be blessed and move on to the next person.

This sign will help build up the faith of the people watching.

THE SECOND SIGN

"If people don't believe this first sign then they will believe the second one."

"God will give you the gift to be able to know secrets hidden in people's hearts. You will know things that have happened to them in the past."

"If you will use these signs carefully and let people know that it is God who is showing you these things, then these signs will grow and grow."

Bill had a lot to think about after this. God wanted to use him for healing.

Now let's just pause for a moment in this story.

If an angel visits you, that does not mean that God is speaking through them. Definite truth is only found in the Bible. The Bible is the only source of truth. If an angel tells you to do something that goes against the Bible, then you know to ignore it.

Some "angels" have spoken to people in the past and have led them to ruin a lot of people's lives. So if an angel comes to you listen carefully and be careful.

On the other hand, angels did speak to people in the past. The angel Gabriel spoke to Mary. Another angel spoke to the shepherds when Jesus was born. Angels can be seen in lots of places in the Bible and stories of angels helping people are known throughout the history of the Church.

What would have happened if Mary had said, "No, this can't be God." How would the shepherds have felt if they hadn't bothered to go and check out what the angel had said?

God is a supernatural God and He can speak in supernatural ways. We don't look for supernatural things to happen—instead we look for God. However, when something supernatural does happen, we need to sit up and pay attention to find out if it really is God speaking.

God warns us about this in Galatians 1:8 *"I pray that God will punish anyone who preaches anything different from our message to you! It doesn't matter if that person is one of us or an angel from heaven."* (CEV)

Here is a key test: Is the focus on Jesus or is it on the fact that *you* saw an angel. If you are thinking about God more and focusing more on telling people about Jesus, then a supernatural sign is a good thing. If you are thinking about the supernatural thing more than God and want to tell people about that sign more than you tell them about Jesus, then something is not right. Of course, if an angel tells you to do something that goes against what God has said in the Bible, then you know to ignore them. That's why God gives us the Bible and each other to help us not mess up along the way.

We will see how for many years God used William Branham to tell other people about Jesus. God did amazing miracles through his ministry. These miracles all helped people to get to know God more. Many people turned to Jesus because of this.

Bill was about to see these signs in action for the first time.

CHAPTER 9

THE NEW ORDER

William Branham

PUT IT INTO PRACTICE

On Sunday Bill told his church about the angel and the first sign God had given to him. As he was speaking, a man came up to him and gave him a note. Bill read the note: "Dear Mr. Branham, my daughter, Betty, is dying. Please come and pray for her. Yours sincerely, Reverend Daugherty."

Reverend Daugherty was a pastor of a church in St. Louis, Missouri. He had heard about what God had done for Bill and he wanted Bill to come and pray.

Betty had been sick for three months. Doctors had come to help her and many people prayed for her, but she did not get better. Betty was very thin and her body would shake on the bed. Everyone could see that she would die soon if she did not have a miracle.

When Bill arrived he prayed for her. She did not get better.

Bill knew that God wanted to heal Betty, but it had not happened. He took time to pray. For three hours he prayed. When he came back to Betty, she was still no better. Bill went off again to pray some more.

After a while he came back. This time he looked different. He had seen a vision and he knew what God wanted him to do.

"Do what I tell you and God will heal Betty. Get some white cloth and water and dab it on her head, hands, and feet. Then kneel and pray with me."

Betty's parents did as Bill asked them to. As Bill prayed, Betty was totally healed. It was an outstanding miracle.

LET'S MEET

When people heard about the miracle they all wanted to meet Bill. Bill wanted to be by himself. He knew he needed time with God if God was going to use him. He promised that he would come back to St. Louis.

On June 14, 1946, he kept his promise. Bill told the people what God had done for him. He then prayed for the sick. A man who had not walked for several years got up and walked out of the building. A man who was blind left the meeting seeing. Several people who were deaf were healed.

The next day Bill was taken to visit an insane woman in a mental hospital. She immediately became normal and was let out of hospital soon after.

Then he went to see a lady who was dying of cancer. She was healed.

In the next home there was a lady who had been half paralyzed for a year. She could not move her right arm or her right leg. She also couldn't talk. After prayer she stood by herself, then started to clap both her hands and praise God as she carefully walked for the first time in a year.

That evening the tent where they were meeting was full. God continued to do amazing miracles. A seventy-year-old lady had a tumor on the end of her nose. One week later she came back and it had gone.

A preacher who had been blind for twenty years was completely healed. Many people knew him. They knew they had witnessed Jesus doing a real miracle, just like the ones Jesus had done in the Bible.

As the nights went on, the crowds got bigger and bigger and the miracles continued to increase. It was like the days of the early church. So many miracles were happening. Like the early church, Bill didn't just pray for the sick; he also invited people to accept Jesus. One lady walked out in disgust and as she walked out, she had a heart attack and fell to the ground. Bill was called out to her. He prayed and she became well. She then told Bill how she had rejected God in that tent. That night, out on the street, she changed her mind. She knew that she had met with the real God. She knew she had to follow Him.

Each night Bill could feel God's love for the people. He did not want to leave until every person had been prayed for. Often he was still awake at 2 o'clock in the morning as he prayed for the sick to be healed. He also prayed with every person who wanted to follow Jesus.

The crusade carried on until Bill got a message asking him to go home and pray for a sick girl.

AMAZING ARKANSAS

In the fall of 1946 Bill headed off for a week in Arkansas. He had been preaching and praying for the sick nonstop. People were being healed, but Bill was exhausted. He knew that after his week in Arkansas he would need a holiday. He didn't realize that he would be even more exhausted after this week.

Over 25,000 people came to hear him. For eight days he prayed for people almost constantly. He ate at the pulpit and slept for a few hours by the pulpit. When he woke there was still a long line of people waiting to be prayed for.

Bill grabbed hold of one lady's hand, just as the angel had told him to. As he did, his hand started to swell and some spots appeared on it. The first time his hand had swollen, Bill had been surprised. Now Bill was learning what the spots meant. He could tell what disease the person had just by looking at the pattern of the spots.

As Bill looked at the pattern on his hand, he knew what was wrong with the lady.

"You have cancer," Bill said.

The lady nodded. She took the handkerchief away from her face. Then Bill saw that her whole nose had been eaten into by the tumor.

"Do you believe God can heal you?"

"I've got no other choice," the lady said, "God is my only hope."

As Bill spoke to her and prayed for her, his hand stopped throbbing. He knew that the lady had been healed.

So the meetings went on. Blind people were healed, and lame people walked. Nobody wanted to leave the tent. Each person who left told of the amazing miracles God was doing. The crowd outside got bigger and bigger.

Bill called Meda, "You've got to come and see the amazing things that God is doing—it is so special."

When Meda arrived she was amazed to see what God was doing. "Look at all these people, Bill. And to think they've all come to see you," Meda said.

"No," Bill replied, "they've all come to see Jesus."

Bill had gone out of the tent to meet Meda. He turned to go back to the tent and realized he had made a big mistake— now he had to go through the huge crowd.

OUTSIDE THE TENT

As they tried to get back into the tent, a man called out to Bill.

"Brother Branham, please help."

"Sir, I can't pray for people out here. If I do it will cause a lot of problems. But if you stand in the line I will pray for you."

"It's not for me. I just drive an ambulance. I think the lady in my ambulance has just died and I can't find a doctor. Please come. If only to speak to her husband—he is devastated."

Bill pushed through the crowd to get to the ambulance.

Once inside he found a lady lying there. She looked like she was not breathing and he could not find a pulse. He held her hand and his hand did not swell up.

"She had cancer," her husband sobbed. "She's had it for years. We spent everything we had on doctors, but she did not get better. Now she wanted you to pray for her, but it's too late."

"Well, the only thing I can do is pray," Bill said, and he started to pray. As he prayed, he felt the lady's hand twitch. He opened his eyes and looked at the lady. She still looked dead.

"It must have been my imagination," he thought and he carried on praying. As he prayed, the lady squeezed his hand. Bill opened his eyes and saw her sitting up. She was totally well.

"Who are you?" the lady asked.

"I am Brother Branham," Bill replied.

When the husband realized that his wife was alive he started to scream out praise to God. A crowd was building up outside the ambulance. People had found out that someone had been healed and knew that Bill must be inside.

Bill had to slip out the side of the ambulance undercover. Most people in the crowd had only heard about him; they had never seen him. As long as he could get away from the ambulance he should be able to get back to the tent without anyone noticing him.

He escaped the ambulance easily, but he did not realize how difficult it would be to get back to the tent. The crowd outside was still growing bigger.

Bill tried to push his way through, but people told him he would have to wait his turn.

Then in the middle of the crowd Bill heard a girl crying, "Daddy, Daddy."

The little girl was lost. Bill went to her.

Then he saw she was blind.

"I can't find my daddy. I want to go home. I came to see the healer," she told Bill.

"How did you hear about him?" Bill asked.

"I was listening to the radio. They were saying that people born deaf and blind were being healed. That's why I came. I want to be healed, but it's the last night and I can't even get into the tent. Now I can't even find the bus to get home."

Bill wept. He was so sorry for this poor girl. "Perhaps I'm the one you're looking for," Bill said.

"Are you the healer? Please pray for me."

"I'm not the healer. Jesus is the healer. I am Brother Branham." Then Bill bowed his head and started to pray.

"I CAN SEE! I CAN SEE!" The girl screamed out.

People realized who Bill was and a crowd gathered round him.

"Brother Branham, please pray for me." One man in the crowd cried out. He was leaning on crutches and his legs were all twisted. For eight hours the man had stood in the rain trying to get inside. Now William Branham was standing right next to him.

"Do you believe God can heal you? Do you believe that God can use me?"

"Yes, I do."

"Then in the name of Jesus Christ you are healed. Throw away your crutches," Bill declared.

Immediately the man's legs became straight.

Everywhere people went they talked about what God was doing through Brother Branham. Bill's ministry was about to grow even faster.

CHAPTER 10

GROWING FAST

William Branham speaking to the crowds

YOU'RE THE MAN

Bill was in California when a man came to speak to him and said, "Excuse me, sir, can you tell me how you spell your name?"

"Sure. It's W-I-L-L-I-A-M B-R-A-N-H-A-M."

"You are the one that God told me about!" the man said. "Twenty-two years ago I was praying when God gave me this word."

He pulled out a piece of paper from his pocket. The paper was so old that it had turned yellow. Bill looked at the paper.

"My servant, William Branham, will come up the West Coast with a gift of divine healing."

That's exactly what Bill was doing!

The more he prayed for people, the more Bill learned about the first sign the angel had told him about. When people came to be prayed for he held their right hand with his left hand, just like the angel had told him to. When he did this his left hand would swell up and marks would appear on it. The worse the disease, the more his hand would swell.

To begin with, Bill did not understand how this sign worked. Then he started to see a pattern. Different diseases made different marks on his hand. But the same diseases always made the same pattern. Before long Bill was able to tell what disease someone had just by looking at the marks on his hand.

Bill knew that this helped people to believe that God had sent him. He wanted people to look to God, not to him. With so many miracles happening in his meetings that wasn't always easy.

Bill soon found that he would be very tired. He met a man called Gordon Lindsay. Gordon loved Jesus and knew that God was using Bill. He could also see that Bill needed help to organize things or he would soon be too exhausted to pray for anybody. Bill wanted to pray for *all* the sick every night. But he was only a human.

Gordon suggested that they made up prayer cards. Then Bill could pray for just a few people each night. Bill hoped that others wanting healing would see the miracles and believe that God could heal them directly without needing Bill to lay hands on them.

STAYING IN THE LINE

February, 1947, Bill was in Phoenix. He felt God telling him to do a fast prayer line that night.

Each person who wanted prayer would walk past Bill as he prayed for them. People walked past rapidly. But with 2500 people to pray for, it still took a long time to pray for everyone.

One man stood in the line with his wife, Haddie Warldorf. Haddie was on a stretcher. She had cancer in her colon and it had spread to her liver and her heart. Haddie knew that she was dying. As she was in the line, she could feel herself passing out.

"Darling," she told her husband, "if I die, stay in the prayer line. I still want to be prayed for."

These were the last words she spoke. A few minutes later she was dead. Her husband did not move. He stayed in the line for over an hour until they reached Bill. When they got to Bill he stopped the prayer line. Taking hold of Haddie's hand, he prayed for her. Immediately she started breathing and sat up. She was too weak to walk to begin with, but by the end of the night she could walk out of the building.

Haddie was not only alive, but she was well. God had taken the cancer away. In fact, she ended up living longer than Bill!

MONEY, MONEY, MONEY

The next month Bill was in Los Angeles. On the second night a lady was carried to him on a stretcher.

Bill took hold of her right hand and felt his hand vibrate.

"It's cancer," Bill announced.

"Yes," a lady replied. "I'm her daughter. She's got breast cancer. This is her doctor. He has done everything he can to help, but it's still spreading. Only God can help her."

Bill bowed his head and prayed. His hand stopped vibrating and he knew that the lady had been healed. He was about to tell the family when something strange happened. He found himself talking.

"In three days this woman will be shopping in the street markets, says the Lord."

Her doctor was outraged. "How can you say that? She is obviously dying. How can you give this woman such hope?"

"Doctor, if that woman is not well in three days, you can put a sign on my back that says I am a false prophet. Then you can drive me around town on the hood of your car."

Bill knew God had healed her. Three days later not even her doctor could deny that God had healed her. By the end of the week Bill was exhausted. He lay on his hotel bed and was about to sleep when there was a knock on the door.

"Sir, we have come from Mr. Melikan." Two men stood at the door.

Bill looked blank. He did not know a Mr. Melikan.

"Mr. Melikan's wife had cancer. On the third day she went shopping with her daughter just like you said she would. Mr. Melikan is so grateful that he sent us here to give you this."

Bill opened up an envelope. Inside it was a check for $1,500,000. The check had his name on it.

Immediately he thought of how it could help his family. Bill had never had much money. With this money he could get water piped into his house. Meda would not have to carry water down the street. They could buy a new house without any draughts. Finally he could give his family a decent home.

There was just one problem. Bill had not healed Mrs. Melikan. Jesus had healed her. How could he take the money when Jesus had done it? Bill knew that money, fame, and women were the three things that Satan often used to stop preachers following God. Many preachers had been ruined by money.

Bill knew he could use the money but he did not wanted to be ruined by it.

"Gentlemen thank you. I do not want to look at that check. Tell Mr. Melikan I appreciate the thought, but I cannot take his money."

CHAPTER 11

THE SECOND SIGN

William Branham and Fred Bosworth

VOICE OF HEALING

Bill wanted a newsletter that would tell people what God was doing. It would not focus on small differences between the churches. Instead it would focus on what God was doing in His Church. Bill spoke to Gordon Lindsay. Gordon could see that Bill's ministry was growing across the nation. Bill gave him the job of writing the newsletter. The *Voice of Healing* newsletter had begun.

A few months later Bill made announcement. "I'm retiring. I'm not going to travel and hold meetings anymore." Often he was praying for people until 2 am. He had lost 40 pounds. His body could not do any more work. He had to stop. He was exhausted.

"It's your fault, Gordon," Bill shouted. "You made me do this crazy schedule. It's your fault I'm ill."

Gordon did not know what to do. Bill was not well, but was it really his fault? He had left his job to travel with Bill. He loved Bill and wanted to help him and protect him. Now Bill was not going anywhere.

Gordon had started the *Voice of Healing* magazine to tell people what God was doing through Bill. Now Bill was not praying for anyone. Gordon could keep the magazine going; he just had to work out what to put in it. He spoke to other healing evangelists who were starting to minister and before long there were over forty ministers who were sharing their stories in the *Voice of Healing* magazine.

While Bill rested, God spoke. "It's now time to use the second sign." Bill knew God was calling him to go out again. This time he was going to be more careful. Gordon would help him not to overwork and to plan his time better. Gordon was a great Bible teacher and Bill had been given a great gift from God. Working together, God would take the ministry to the next level. There was one more key person that God wanted to add to the team.

Fred Bosworth had been praying for the sick for many years. He had met Charles Parham (whose story is told in book 6 of this series) and had been changed by the Holy Spirit back in 1906. Since that time Bosworth had been serving Jesus. By the time Bosworth joined the team, he was an old man.

With the team complete, it was time for the second sign.

THE SIGN OF SECRETS

"You will know the secrets in people's hearts."

That's what the angel had told him. This would be the second sign that God would give him to help him show people that God wants to heal them.

In 1949, Bill was in Canada holding meetings. He was on the platform praying for people. As he stood there, a lady came and stood in front of him. Bill watched the lady and she seemed to shrink in front of him. Where she stood he could now see a twelve-year-old girl. Bill said what he was seeing. The girl was sitting in a school room when a pen flew across the room and hit her in the eye.

"That was me," the lady screamed.

Bill had been having a vision. Now, as the lady screamed, he could see her standing in front of him again.

"That was me. I'm blind in my right eye. The pen hit me there and I have been blind ever since."

God had given Bill a word of knowledge. Bill prayed for the lady and she was healed.

After that day God showed Bill all kinds of visions. Sometimes he knew their names and their addresses. He had never met these people before. God spoke to him and told him these details.

Sometimes God showed Bill people's sins. When this happened Bill usually pushed the microphone away and told them what he had seen. Bill knew that he could only see sins that people had not confessed to God. He did not want to embarrass people. Instead he wanted to help them to get right with God.

Bill had had many visions in his life. Now God was using this gift of words of knowledge to help other people.

INSTRUCTIONS FROM GOD

"Where is he?"

Gordon and his team were panicking. They could not find Bill anyone. He said he was going to arrive in the afternoon, but by the evening they had not heard anything. They hadn't even told him where his hotel was.

They had learned that if people found out where Bill would be staying then hundreds of people would go to the hotel. The hotels weren't happy when this happened and they knew Bill needed to sleep. The only person who knew where Bill would be staying was Reverend Grant. Bill was supposed to speak to him to find out about the hotel, but he hadn't.

Gordon and the team could not think what else they could do. In those days cell phones had not been invented so there was no way to contact Bill, they would have to wait for him to contact them. While they waited to hear from him they decided to go to the hotel. When they got to the hotel they found that Bill had already turned up, checked in, and gone to bed.

The next morning Gordon had to ask, "Bill, how did you know where the hotel was? Reverend Grant was the only one who knew and he didn't tell you."

"I was really tired when I came. I just seemed to know where the hotel was, so I came here and went straight to bed."

Bill didn't have to be in a meeting to hear God speaking to him. He listened to God all the time.

GOING OUT FOR BREAKFAST

One day Bill woke up in his hotel and went out to get some breakfast. He started walking towards the restaurant. Then he stopped.

"Turn left."

Bill knew that God was speaking to him. This time it was not a voice out loud, it was God's voice speaking inside him. Bill turned left and walked down the street. As he walked along he came to a café. He knew this was where they were supposed to be.

The café was crowded. As Bill sat down to eat, the lady sitting at the table next to him cried out, "Praise God."

She then walked over to Bill and spoke: "Brother Branham, I hope you don't mind me interrupting, but I think God has brought you here to see me."

Bill was ready to listen. God was up to something.

"My brother and I came all the way from Texas. My brother is dying. His heart has grown bigger and doctors say there is nothing else they can do to help him. We've been to ten meetings so far but we have never been able to get into the prayer line. Now we have run out of money and have to go home."

"Last night I was so desperate that I prayed all night. I heard God telling me to come to Miller's café for 9 o'clock. If I did that, then he would be healed."

Bill looked at his watch. It was exactly 9 o'clock. Bill walked over to pray for her brother. As he held the man's hand, his own hand swelled up. When he had finished praying his hand had gone back to normal. The man had been healed.

Everyone in the café was amazed. Bill knew he had to leave the café before the crowds started to crush him. As he stepped outside, a woman looked at him in shock.

She grabbed hold of his leg and started to cry, "Thank you, God."

Bill placed his hand on her shoulder, "Stand up, dear sister, and tell me what is wrong."

"I have cancer. The doctors have treated me but the tumor keeps growing. I have prayed and prayed that God would heal me. This morning as I was waking up I had a dream. God was telling me to stand in front of Miller's Café ten minutes after nine o'clock. I tried to get into the prayer lines at your meeting but there were too many other people. Now here you are!"

Bill prayed for her and felt she had been healed. As Bill walked away he could feel that the angel was near him again.

"Now what do you want me to do, Lord?" Bill asked.

This time Bill heard a voice speaking out loud: "Go down to the end of the block, cross the street, and stand there."

As Bill stood there, he saw a lady crossing the road. He knew that was the person God wanted him to meet. He stood the other side of the crossing and she walked past him. Bill was not sure what to do next. The lady was walking away. Then she stopped, turned around, and came back. She was shocked to see Bill standing there.

"Brother Branham, I came to your meetings but could not stand in the prayer line. I was on my way home when I felt God telling me to turn around. When I did I saw you standing there."

The lady had a crippled arm. Bill knew what God wanted him to do. He spoke to her clearly, "Stretch out your arm in the name of Jesus."

The lady stretched out her arm and it was healed.

For nearly an hour he stood on the street praying for sick people who were passing by. Bill finally made it back to the hotel and realized he still hadn't had breakfast, but he had seen God do some amazing miracles.

Even when Bill was at home life was busy. He was getting 1000 letters a day. Many of them were people asking him to pray for them. Some of them were inviting him to come and speak to them. With so much attention it is not surprising that some people were against him.

CHAPTER 12

THE PHOTOGRAPH

William Branham with a light above him

THE CHALLENGE

Fred Bosworth was a great help to Bill. He often spoke in the afternoon meetings, teaching people about healing, using his great knowledge of the Bible and his years of experience in asking God to heal the sick. This helped prepare people's hearts for the evening meeting when Bill would minister. It also meant Bill could take time to rest.

God was bringing back teaching on supernatural healing. Many people were listening to the teaching but not everyone agreed with it.

In January of 1950, Bill and his team traveled to Texas to hold some meetings. After a few days the local newspaper carried a challenge from a local minister called Dr. Best: "William Branham is a crazy fanatic. He is a fake minister and a false prophet. We need to drive him out of town and I am going to do it."

Bosworth showed the paper to Bill. "Bill, you should do it. You should show him what the Bible says about healing."

"God sent me to pray for the sick, not to argue with people who don't agree with me," Bill replied.

That was the end of the conversation—until the next day.

Dr. Best had received no reply from Bill. Now he paid for another advertisement in the paper. This time his words were even stronger: "William Branham is scared of the truth. He is scared to look at divine healing in the Bible. He knows I am right. He knows I would point out how he is wrong."

Bill turned to Bosworth. "Eight thousand people are coming to the meetings each night. Seven thousand of these want to be prayed for. Why should I spend time speaking to this one man."

"These eight thousand people are reading this paper. Some of them wonder if Dr. Best is right. If you won't speak out from the Bible, then let me do it."

Bill looked at the seventy-three-year-old pioneer of the Gospel. He still had the fire of God on him. He still wanted to serve God.

"Okay, Bosworth, you can. Don't get into an argument with him, just preach the Gospel."

Bosworth rushed outside to go and tell the reporters. The papers loved the story and soon people were rushing from across the country to come and hear the debate.

THE DEBATE

The building they had been using had 30,000 seats. On the night of the debate every seat was taken.

Bill sat at home. He did not plan to go to the debate. After all, he believed we should live God's Word, not argue about it. But the longer he sat at home, the more he felt that he needed to be there. Bill entered the building unnoticed.

He and Meda found the last two seats right at the very top of the building. Bill pulled his coat up around his face so no one would recognize him and sat back to listen.

Fred Bosworth stood behind the pulpit and welcomed the people.

"Dr. Best, I have pages and pages of Scriptures here. Each one proves that God is a healer and is healing today. If you can show that even one of them is not about healing I will agree I am wrong and walk off this platform."

"Carry on, Reverend Bosworth. Use up your thirty minutes, then I will speak." Dr. Best replied.

Bosworth tried to get Dr. Best to answer his challenge on the Scriptures, but he refused. So Bosworth started to teach through the Scriptures. Jesus who saves is also Jesus who heals. Jesus is the same yesterday, today, and forever. God healed in the Old Testament, He healed in the New Testament, and He still heals people today.

He ran out of time before he had even gone through half of his Scriptures.

Dr. Best stood up and started to teach using just one passage of the Bible. "The most important thing is that people are saved. They do not need to be healed," he thundered. When he finished, it was obvious who was teaching more clearly from the Bible. The people did not believe Dr. Best.

Dr. Best was angry. "Only holy-rollers believe this. No true Baptist would believe in healing."

Bosworth stepped up to the microphone and said, "Just a moment, Dr. Best. I want to ask the people something. Bosworth turned to the crowd and said, "If you are a true Baptist and you can prove with a doctor's letter that you have been healed by Jesus, please stand up."

Three hundred people stood up.

"Anyone can stand up; that doesn't make it true," Dr. Best blurted.

"I have shown you from the Word and now you can see it from people's testimony. How can you keep saying God does not heal people?"

Dr. Best knew that he had lost the argument. He still wanted to be able to report back in the papers the next day. So he called his photographers to come and take photos of him arguing. He posed and wagged a finger under Fred Bosworth's nose.

The photographers snapped away. These photos would make him look like the winner in tomorrow's paper.

Dr. Best ended his argument saying, "The big question is: Where is the healer? Where is William Branham? Why is he not here?"

"Hold on a minute, Dr. Best." Bosworth replied. "William Branham is not a healer. He is just a preacher who preaches that Jesus heals."

"He is the healer. That's what people say," Dr. Best replied.

"Do you preach that Jesus is the Savior?" Bosworth asked.

"Yes, I do." Dr. Best replied.

"Does that make you the Savior of people?" replied Bosworth.

"Of course not! Jesus is the one who saves," Dr. Best retorted.

"William Branham preaches Jesus as the Savior and the Healer of people," Bosworth replied.

"Well, where is he then?" Dr. Best asked, sarcastically.

"He's in this building. I saw him slip in. I don't mind if he wants to close this meeting—that is up to him."

Meda nudged Bill, "Don't go, Bill." Bill didn't plan to move.

Then he heard the sound of the whirlwind. The angel was close to him. God wanted him to go.

"God wants me there," Bill said. With that, he stood up and walked to the front.

"I'm sorry this debate had to happen. Nobody feels badly towards Dr. Best. He has the right to believe what he wants to just like I am free to believe what I want to...."

Bill looked up in the balcony. He saw a light there. He had seen a light in a lot of his meetings. God often pointed out people who He was healing with a light. Now Bill watched the light.

As he stood there, a stillness came over the crowd. Many saw a light flash from the balcony to the front. It happened so quickly that people were not sure if it was real or just their imagination.

One of the photographers jumped up and took a photo of Bill.

The meeting was over.

DEVELOPING THE PHOTOGRAPHS

The two photographers headed home. It had been a fun night and they had taken loads of great photos. One of them was a Jew; the other had been brought up as a Catholic. Neither of them really believed in God. Both of them had enjoyed the evening, though.

There had been something different in the room.

"I'm going to straight to bed," one of the photographers said.

"I'm going to develop the film. I know Dr. Best will want some photos for tomorrow's paper."

It took a while for the photos to be seen from the film and the photographer wanted to have the photos ready.

When he looked at the first photo, he knew he had a problem. It was completely blank. There was nothing on it.

The second photo was exactly the same. So was the third. In fact all of the photos had come out blank. The only one that had survived was the one of William Branham.

As the photographer watched the photo appearing he noticed a mark above William Branham's head. It was like a circle of light. It looked like a halo.

The photographer was at a loss for words. This was a miracle. He had seen a light in the building; now he could see the same light hovering over Bill's head.

The next morning he sent a copy of the photo to Bill. Bill was pleased. God was looking after him.

"Of course this is not the first time the light has been seen on a photo," Fred Bosworth said. "In the past people have said the photo was altered or touched up in some way."

"Well, we won't let them do that this time," Gordon Lindsey chipped in. "We'll get proof."

George Lacy worked for the FBI. It was his job to look at documents and photos to see if they were fake or if they were real. All this took place before the days of modern computers when it is now easy to add things onto a digital photo. This photo had been taken on old-fashioned film. Gordon sent a copy of the photo to him.

A few days later he met with Bill. "I had heard about you. I thought you were just tricking people's minds into believing. But the camera cannot be tricked. I have done every test available to us today and I am sure that light was really there."

George Lacy told the papers what he had found and gave a copy of his report to Bill to use as needed. Several weeks after that event many people told about their experience in the meeting. Many of them had seen the light. When they saw the photo they were amazed. The photograph was so clear. It was just as they had seen it.

God was using William Branham, and soon even more people would hear about what God was doing.

CHAPTER 13

AROUND THE WORLD

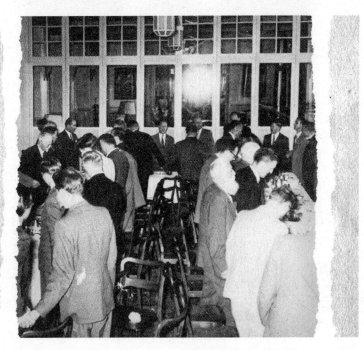

Ministering in Switzerland

FAMOUS HEALING

William Upshaw was very well known in America. He was a preacher, a teacher and an author. But most people knew him as a Congressman. He was even put forward as a candidate to be the President of the United States.

Everyone knew him as the congressman who needed crutches to walk.

When Congressman Upshaw was eighteen years old he was working on a farm. As he worked, he fell off a wagon and landed on his back. His back was broken and he could not walk. Young William Upshaw had just come to know Jesus. Now he turned to Jesus and asked Him to heal him. Each time he went for prayer the Holy Spirit seemed to say,

"Not yet."

William still kept praying and asking others to pray for him. For the next seven years he was confined to his bed. Then he started to use the crutches to move around. He went through his life teaching people, "Let nothing discourage you. Never give up!" As they saw him carrying on with life with crutches, they were encouraged to keep going.

When he became a congressman he was able to help the country. His wife prayed that he would be healed so that he could preach the Gospel more easily. After fifty-nine years of walking on crutches and praying to God he was still not healed.

Then, at the age of 84, in February, 1951, he went to a William Branham meeting. For sixty-six years he had been asking God to heal him. As he walked in to the tent, he wondered if tonight was his night. His wife was praying next to him. People all around him were being healed.

William Branham was being carried off the platform. He had been praying for many people and was now too tired to go on. William Upshaw remembered what his wife would often say, "When you lead some to Jesus you tell them to accept Him and step out, then the feeling will follow."

William Upshaw stood up and decided to try a step. He did not feel anything. Just then William Branham spoke out, "The congressman is being healed."

Now Congressman William Upshaw knew this was a word from God. Strength came into his legs and for the first time in sixty-six years he started to walk without his crutches. Everyone could see that God had healed him. It was a true miracle and nobody could deny it.

GO TO THE NATIONS

The *Voice of Healing* magazine had traveled around the world and now Bill started to travel outside of America too. Everywhere he went people were amazed to see God at work. Bill traveled to South Africa and saw God do many miracles there, but not everything was easy.

In South Africa the black people were not treated like people. The white people had their own buses, their own schools and their own ways of doing things and they were in charge. Bill wanted to see all people come to know Jesus.

Here in South Africa black and white people were not even allowed to sit in the same room.

When Jesus walked on the Earth He loved the leaders but He also loved the servants. He loved everybody and spent time with everyone. At that time, however, Jesus' church in South Africa did not copy Jesus. They were no different from the rest of the country.

Bill had been invited out by white preachers. All the people in the churches he went to were white. He longed to preach to the black people—after all, there were far more black people than white people in South Africa.

After twenty-one days in the country, he finally had a chance to speak to them. Twelve thousand people came to the first meeting for the natives. Ern Baxter, one of Bill's team, preached the Gospel, then Bill started to pray for the sick.

One bus driver was shocked. One of his passengers had been carried into the meeting, and now they came out walking. Blind eyes were opened. Deaf people were healed. Cancers disappeared. The people there had much trust in God.

Bill loved being with these people of faith. He knew they were his brothers and sisters even if they weren't allowed to come to his other meetings. Bill had had to beg the organizers to let him be with his black brothers and sisters because he wanted to spend all his time with them.

EUROPE

Bill also traveled across Europe. In the United Kingdom it is said that William Branham prayed for King George VI of England and God healed him. In Finland, he saw a boy in a serious car accident recover. In Portugal and Italy God moved powerfully. In Switzerland and Germany many people became Christians.

The government in Norway tried to ban Bill from praying for the sick. Bill knew that if he did pray for the sick he would be kicked out of the country. The Church in Norway was not happy. Jesus had prayed for the sick and since the time of Jesus the Church had always prayed for people who were sick. Two hundred ministers got together and wrote to the government. The letter was signed by some of the top church leaders of the day. The Church in Norway was standing together and standing up for God's Kingdom.

Bill was at the very front of this move of God and had a big part to play at this time. He was not the only person God was using. Many other great people were also being raised up.

INDIA

By the time Bill arrived in Bombay, India, people had heard what God was doing around the world through Bill. Now the people wanted to see for themselves.

At the first meeting over 300,000 people came.

The first person Bill prayed for was a child who could not speak or hear. Bill clapped his hands and the boy jumped. For the first time in his life he spoke into the microphone. Everybody knew they had seen a miracle.

The people rushed forward to see Bill. The meeting was about to turn into a riot and had to stop.

The next day religious leaders from different religions asked to meet with Bill. Each one had a question for him. Bill told them how Jesus had died for them and he invited them all to come to the meeting that night.

To his surprise, they all came.

The roads to the meeting place were so full of crowds going to the meeting that it took Bill two hours to get to the meeting.

As he walked up to the pulpit, he saw several rows of police officers standing at the front. They were there to stop the people from rushing forward again. On the very front row sat the religious leaders he had met earlier in the day.

Bill looked around the room. He had seen lots of insects in India and he knew just how he could tell these people about Jesus.

"A bee has only one sting. Once it has stung it cannot do anything else. Sin is like a bee trying to sting us. When we sin, that sin harms us, but Jesus took the sting for us. When Jesus died on the Cross He was taking all our sin away."

When it was time to pray for the sick a blind man was brought to Bill. The blind man was forced to sit on the street and beg for food and money. As he came near to Bill, Bill saw a vision. In the vision he saw the man as a boy who could see. Then he saw the man worshiping the sun. The man looked at the sun for so long that he had gone blind. After that Bill saw the man standing with his family in the vision.

Bill told the audience what he had seen and the blind man said it was all true. Bill got ready to pray for the man. He did not know whether or not God would heal him. Looking at the man, he could only see white in his eyes. There was no way he could see without a miracle. Bill knew God could do miracles, but God had not shown him anything.

As he was about to pray, Bill saw another vision. In this vision he was laying his hand on the man and praying for him to be healed in the name of Jesus. Now Bill knew that the man would be healed. He turned to the crowd and looked at the men on the front row.

"People from the different religions here in India, you can see this blind man. You Moslems want to make him a Moslem. You Buddhists want to make him a Buddhist. You Sikhs want to make him a Sikh. That's just changing people's thinking. But the God who made this man can heal him. So which god is real? Do you agree to follow the God who can heal this man?"

The crowd roared. In India there are many religions, but these people wanted the truth. Bill turned to the religious leaders. "If your god can heal him please come forward now and show us."

They did not move.

"They cannot do this." Bill said. "But Jesus Christ can. Jesus saves us from sin and He heals us. He showed me a vision. This man will be healed. If he is not healed, you can kick me out of India and call me a fake. If he is healed, do you agree to follow Jesus?"

Again the crowd roared their agreement. Bill placed his hand over the beggar's eyes and prayed, "In the name of Jesus give this man his sight that many people will believe in you."

As Bill took his hand away, the man ran forward and hugged him. "I can see! I can see!"

Then he turned and hugged the mayor of the town. The crowd knew they had seen the one true God working a miracle in front of them. They had seen lots of magic, but they had never seen anything like this before.

The policemen at the front of the crowd could not hold the people back. Once again Bill had to escape from the meeting before the crowds crushed him.

Half-a-million people had been saved and even more had been healed through William Branham's ministry at that time.

God was doing incredible things, but Bill was about to go off course.

CHAPTER 14

A TWIST IN THE TALE

William Branham standing alone

SEPARATION

In 1951, Gordon Lindsay decided to leave Bill. He had helped Bill get organized and had been a Bible teacher. However, during this time Bill had often blamed Gordon for getting or doing things wrong.

After Gordon left, the IRS claimed that Bill had not paid his tax. Bill was only on a small salary and had paid all the tax on that. But he had not paid tax on the money people gave him, which he then gave to the ministry. He owed the IRS $40,000.

Bit by bit, Bill started to pay it off. He wanted to honor God in every part of his life. He just need help to do that.

He really needed someone like Gordon to help him. God had sent Gordon to work with Bill for that very reason, but Bill never really appreciated everything that Gordon did for him. This was probably the biggest mistake of Bill's ministry.

Gordon and Bill made a great team. Gordon was a great teacher. Bill had been given a supernatural gift from God. The two men needed each other.

When God uses you to do amazing things you have to be a strong and selfless person not to think that you are the one who is great. Whatever God does through you does not make you better than other people. It is only because of Jesus that anybody can stand in God's presence. It is only Jesus' love for us that allows us to be used by Him.

Nobody is perfect. We need to remember that. If we do, then we will love everyone else as our fellow human beings. When we start to think that we know everything and have everything right, then we are in danger of messing up.

When Gordon left Bill, Bill messed up.

Gordon was able to say no to Bill. When Gordon left, everyone around Bill was so amazed by the gift that God had given him that they agreed with whatever he said and did.

TEACHING

Bill had not focused on in-depth, detailed teaching before. He wanted everyone to feel welcome in his meetings, and he did not want to see the Church divided. So, now he decided he wanted to teach people. This was the opposite of what he had been doing.

"I'll only teach people in my home church," he told people. "When I travel, I will stick to the basics."

That's great in theory. But when people heard they could get recordings of his teachings, they did, and his teachings started to spread.

Some of the things he taught were strange, and as the people heard what Bill was saying in his recorded teachings, less and less people went to his meetings.

Bill blamed it on the people. "These people don't want to follow God. God is going to judge the Church because of this." He should have looked at what he was doing wrong. Instead he said there was something wrong with the people who did not agree with him.

He taught that all women were evil. He taught that there was something special in the shape of a pyramid. He said that all teaching about the doctrine of the Trinity, the Godhead, God the Father, Christ Jesus the Son, and the Holy Spirit was wrong.

A lot of his teaching focused on the last days of Jesus. When Bill was younger he had been given prophecies that he was called to get things ready for Jesus' Second Coming. As he prayed for the sick and showed people God's glory, he helped to get Church ready.

Now he thought that these prophecies had an extra special meaning. And so did his followers.

"Names that end in –HAM are very important," William Branham preached. "AbraHAM has seven letters in his name. Billy GraHAM is being used by God to win many people to Jesus. His name ends in –HAM, but he only has six letters in his name."

When people heard him say this it did not take much to figure out that William BranHAM had seven letters in his name. Bill was getting people to look at him, instead of at Jesus. Something had changed in his ministry.

He may not have meant it that way, but lots of people saw it that way.

WHO IS HE?

"He is Jesus—He is the Messiah."

William Branham heard that some of his church believed this. He was devastated. How could they possibly think he was the one who saved them? He spent the whole of his life trying to point people to Jesus and now they were confused— they thought he was Jesus!

William Branham was quick to tell people that he was not the Messiah.

When they gave him other names, he did not disagree with them. In fact, sometimes when he was teaching it sounded like he really believed what they had said.

"You are Elijah!" they said. "You are 'the end time' prophet in the last days."

Bill told his followers about a third ministry God would give him. His other ministries had been in public, this one would be in a small tent by the side of the meetings. Bill was being given a special power from God. He even said that he just had to speak and anything he wanted to happen would happen.

Some people said this was because his mouth had been specially formed by God. Only he could say God's name

"Jehovah" properly—and that's why God listened to him so he could make something appear out of nothing. This, of course, is quite ridiculous. Of course God can answer our prayers. He sees our faith and responds. (Jesus tells us we can even cast a mountain into the sea if we have enough faith). [See Matthew 21:21.].

He then told them that God had sent him to make a big announcement. He was to say that the seven seals in Revelation were being opened. [See Revelation 5:5.] As Bill's claims about himself got bigger, his love for people seemed to grow smaller.

Bill was used by God to heal the sick and give amazing words of knowledge. He was not a prophet, because many of his prophecies did not come true. Now Bill was spending more and more time looking at these strange things. His followers believed him, but the rest of the Church looked on and felt sorry for him.

The people In Canada did not respond to him. In reply, William spoke words of judgment against them. The man who had so much love for people and accepted everyone was now judging people. Something major had changed. William and his followers thought it was God; everyone else could tell that it wasn't.

The problem was that miracles were still happening. This is no surprise. When God gives a gift He does not take it back again. People saw the miracles and believed that everything Bill said must be from God. Jesus even warns us that this will happen.

The question was what would happen now? William Branham was making great mistakes, but still able to do great signs and wonders. There was a real danger that he could lead many people the wrong way.

WARNING

A young evangelist called Kenneth Hagin had been inspired by William Branham's ministry. In 1964, Kenneth Hagin was praying with some friends when God spoke this prophecy through him:

"At the end of 1965, the person who is standing as a prophet at the front of the healing ministry will be taken away. He is getting into error. Satan will destroy his life. He will be saved and his works will follow him."

Kenneth Hagin knew that a word like this had to be judged by other believers. He went to see Gordon Lindsay. When Kenneth Hagin left, Gordon looked at his wife, Freda. She spoke first and said: "Is this about Brother Branham?"

"Yes, it is." Gordon replied. "He thinks he is Elijah. It's sad but people are putting words into his mouth."

Four times Gordon Lindsay was told by prophets that William Branham was going to die and that he had to tell Bill this.

Gordon kept trying to get to William through all of his advisors but they did not let him get close to Bill. Gordon kept trying until finally he managed to get to his old friend Bill by showing up without warning.

Gordon reasoned with and encouraged his friend and brother in the Lord and said, "Bill, why don't you stay and do what God wants you to do. God's given you a gift. Use it. Stay there! Stop trying to be a teacher, that's not what God has called you to do."

Bill shrugged his shoulders, "Yeah, but I want to teach."

With only eighteen months left until the end of 1965 it wouldn't be long before they would find out if this prophecy was from God.

CHAPTER 15

THE ACCIDENT

William Branham with Meda and their children

ON THE WAY HOME

Bill had just preached at a friend's church. He was now driving through Texas on their way to Indiana. It was a long drive, but Bill had done it lots of times before. It was December 18, 1965.

Bill's son, Billy Paul, was leading the way. Billy Paul's wife and younger brother were in his car. Bill drove behind them with Meda and their daughter, Sarah. It was a dark night and with no street lights on the road, they needed their car lights to see where they were going.

Billy Paul went around a corner and saw a single light coming towards him. It looked like the light of a motorbike. As he got nearer he realized that it was a car with only one headlight working.

The car was driving in the middle of the road and was heading straight for them. Billy Paul swerved to one side and just missed a crash. As he looked back, he saw the car swerving across the road. "That driver is crazy," he thought. "I hope dad will be okay."

Then he heard a loud crash. It sounded like an explosion.

Billy Paul looked around and felt sick. That car had smashed into his dad's car. Billy Paul turned the car around and went back up the road. He stopped, got out of the car, and ran straight to the accident. Both cars were wrecks and there was blood and glass everywhere.

Bill had gone through the windshield and was now lying half in, half out of the car.

"Dad, Dad! Are you okay?"

Bill looked up at him and opened his eyes.

"Can you get me out of here?"

"I don't think so, but just speak the word, dad, and you'll be free."

Bill said nothing.

Billy Paul's wife trembled, "Billy Paul. Look! Your mom! She's—she's dead."

Billy Paul rushed around to the other side of the car. She had no pulse.

"Where is she?" Bill asked.

"Just down to your right."

"Take my hand and put it on her," Bill said.

Bill was in pain, but when his hand touched Meda he prayed, "Lord, please heal her. Don't leave these children without their mommy." Immediately Meda groaned and moved. She was alive again.

Before long the mess of glass, oil, smashed cars and blood was surrounded by police and paramedics. They carried Meda and Sarah out of the car and rushed them to hospital. Bill was stuck in the car. His body seemed to have been squashed into the door. They knew they had to get him out fast if he was going to live.

They attached two trucks to each end of the car and pulled slowly. At last there was a gap big enough to free Bill from the car. He was badly injured.

IN THE HOSPITAL

In the hospital they found that Sarah had broken her back. She had cuts on her face too, but she was alive and would get better. Meda was bruised and cut with many broken bones. She also had a concussion. It did not look good.

Bill was in the worst condition. He needed to be intensive care, which meant he had to go to a different hospital, but he was too sick to travel. First he had to have a blood transfusion. They would have to work on him until he was stable enough to be moved.

When they thought he was well enough to go on to the next hospital, he went by ambulance. There they had all the right equipment to take care of him.

Word went around the world. "Brother William Branham and his family have been seriously injured." Soon many Christians were praying for him. Many of his friends and family came to the hospital to pray.

As the days went by, Meda was getting better, but Bill was not. He had many broken bones and they were starting to line up again, but his eyes were swelling up. That meant his brain must be swelling. He needed an operation fast or his brain would be squeezed and he would be dead.

Billy Paul agreed to the operation. The swelling went down, but Bill did not wake up. At 4:37 in the morning he stopped breathing. The nurse attached him to a machine to help him breathe. His heart was still beating.

The doctors were doing everything they could, but it was not enough. The crash was too great and God was calling William Branham home.

On Friday December 24, at 5:49 in the afternoon Bill Branham died.

LIFE AFTER DEATH

William Branham's followers were in shock. They thought Jesus would come back while William Branham was still alive. If Bill was dead, how could Jesus return? Many of them believed God would raise William from the dead.

Meda was not ready to bury him yet. Hadn't Bill said that Jesus would come back at Easter time? Meda didn't even know where or when she was going to bury her husband.

She waited 108 days. Easter of 1966 went past and Bill did not come back to life. So on April 11, 1966, William

Branham was buried. Even then some of Bill's followers believed that Bill would come alive again at Easter time. Predictions like that are not found in the Bible.

William Branham's teachings are spread by those who listen to and follow his teachings. Today they send thousands of his messages around the world for people to listen to. These people are known as followers of "the Message."

Today it is thought that around two million people are followers of William Branham's teachings. Not all of them believe everything that he taught is right, but they all respect his life and his ministry and they want to follow the Bible teachings carefully.

William Branham's greatest legacy was not his teaching or his prophecies about the end times. Some of these were from God. Others were clearly confused, especially as he came near the end of his life.

What William did leave behind was the message about a God who heals and saves today. He showed people that "Jesus Christ is the same yesterday, today, and forever."

Many Christians now believe and expect God to heal today because of Branham's ministry. God had used him to head up a movement during the 1940s and 1950s.

Many ministers went home to their churches and changed the way that they ministered after seeing God work through William Branham. Some of them became famous; many did not. The list of well-known ministers who were affected by Branham is many. To name a few:

- O.L. Jaggers
- Gayle Jackson
- Velmer Gardner
- Richard Vineyard
- Richard Jeffries
- H. Richard Hall
- Tommy L. Osborn
- W.V. Grant, Jr.
- Neal Frisby

The other great healing evangelist of the time, Oral Roberts, also knew and was impacted by William Branham. In fact, many of the healing revivalists can trace some link back to his ministry in the early days of God's move of healing on the Earth.

It is impossible to know how many people were changed by the message of divine healing through his life. It is clear that God used him. It is also clear that the Church is now more ready for Jesus to come back than it was before

William Branham started preaching and showing God's power to heal.

As with all people who follow God, he made mistakes, especially at the end of his life. But he let God use him and many people saw more of God because of him.

STAY IN YOUR CALLING

William Branham was called by God to help prepare the Church for Jesus coming back. This is really the call of all ministers. Jesus tells us we need to be ready for when He comes back.

William Branham did a lot of things right. He did *not* get tripped up by money. He *did* love people. He did *not* try to argue with people. He turned to Jesus when hard things happened and everyone who knew him could see he was a humble man who loved God. But he was not perfect.

William Branham was not called as a teacher; he was called as someone who would demonstrate God's super-natural power of healing. When William worked as part of a team that included organizers and teachers his ministry was strengthened. When he tried to do everything by himself things started to go wrong. The people were misled when Bill started to teach and He missed it when he pushed people away that God had put around him. However, God does not take His gifts away from us when He has given them, even if we make mistakes. [See Romans 11:29.]

When God gives you a job to do don't worry about how great it looks. Instead, make sure that you do what God tells you to do. Don't do anything more or anything less. It's important for us to know *what* God wants us to do. It's also important that we know *when* He wants us to do it.

Some people know what God has called them to do from when they are young. Many people have to wait years before they find out. While they wait they don't stand around idly waiting; instead, they get on with living for Jesus with all their heart: Loving other people and telling them about Jesus.

Do you know what you are called to do? Why not ask God to show you? Ask God to get you ready. As God trains you, don't follow your own ideas and don't do things just because other people tell you what to do. Instead study the Bible and follow God's call for your life.

You are the only person who is called to be you! Only you are called to do what God wants you to do. If we spend our time doing what God has called others to do, not only will we miss what He has for us, but we may get in the way of others who want to serve God. Worse still, we may confuse others and damage how people understand and see God, even though we don't mean to.

Decide today to follow God 100% of the time as best as you possibly can. Hang around with the right people. If you mess up, come back to God and carry on living for Him.

Go, and do great things for God, in Jesus' name!

BIBLE STUDY FOR YOUNG GENERALS

Read 1 Corinthians 12:12-26.

1. Who is part of the Body of Christ (verse 13)?
2. Who decides what part of the Body we should be (verse 18)?
3. Who is the most important person in the Body (verse 25)?
4. How should we treat the parts of God's Body that we think are less important (verse 22-23)?
5. When you think about William Branham's life what part do you think he had to play in the Body of Christ?
6. What can you do to remind yourself that you need others to do what God has called you to do?

Towards the end of his life, William Branham judged people more and loved them less. Pray through each part of 1 Corinthians 13 that God will help you to really love other people (even the ones who annoy you!).

WILLIAM BRANHAM —ACTIVITY SECTION

REMEMBER THE BOOK

How much of the story can you remember? Test your memory by answering these questions.

Answers are given on page 124.

1. When Billy gave his life to Jesus what did he see?
2. How old was Bill when he was ordained as a minister?
3. What was Bill's 2nd wife called?
4. Who helped to organize Bill's campaigns?
5. What was the second sign God gave Bill?
6. How did William Branham die?

CHOOSE THE RIGHT ANSWER

Answers are given on page 124.

1. How did God first speak to Billy?
    A. By an angel
    B. Through the Bible
    C. An audible voice in a tree

2. Who first told Billy about Jesus?
    A. A ranch hand
    B. A preacher
    C. His parents

3. What was Bill's 1st wife called?
    A. Faith
    B. Hope
    C. Love

4. How did Bill know if God had healed someone after he had prayed?
    A. The person would fall down
    B. A doctor would see
    C. His hand would go back to normal

5. What newsletter did Bill start?

   A. Branham's Ministry

   B. The Voice of Healing

   C. The Sinner's Prayer

6. What did Bill do that God had not called him to do (but had called others to do)?

   A. He became a doctor

   B.

   C. He focussed on teaching

AROUND THE WORLD

Bill Branham travelled to lots of places. Time yourself to find out how quickly can you find these countries on a world map *in the order they are written:*

1. America
2. South Africa
3. United Kingdom
4. Norway
6. Portugal
7. India
8. Switzerland
9. Germany

Write down your times here.

Date	Time Taken

PUZZLE IT

Fit these words into the grid to the right.

- 3 letters: See, Way
- 4 letters: Bill, Halo, Hope, Love, Pray
- 5 letters: Cross, Jesus
- 6 letters: Church
- 7 letters: Branham, Healing, Revival, William
- 9 letters: Anointing, Salvation
- 10 letters: Holy Spirit

Answers are given on page 128.

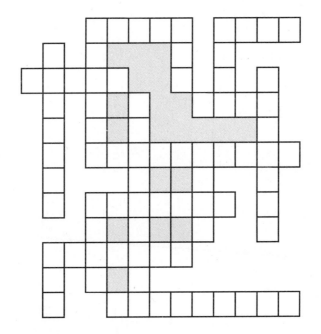

ANSWERS

	C	R	O	S	S		H	O	P	E
H		H			E		A			
J	E	S	U	S		E		L		R	
A		R		S			L	O	V	E
L		C		A						V
I		H	O	L	Y	S	P	I	R	I	T
N			V			R				V
G		B	R	A	N	H	A	M		A
		I		T			Y			L
W	I	L	L	I	A	M			
A		L		O					
Y			A	N	O	I	N	T	I	N	G

FIND IT OUT

William Branham was given a sign from God to let him know if people had been healed or not. Signs point us in the right direction, showing us something that may be hidden. In Science there are many indicators used to test for different things. One indicator measures the pH of substances (how acidic something is).

You can make your own home-made pH indicator.

YOU WILL NEED

- A red cabbage.
- A saucepan.
- Boiling water.
- Small pots.
- Food types to test. For example, lemon juice, apple juice, water, baking soda.

WHAT TO DO

1. Tear up pieces of red cabbage and put them in a saucepan.
2. Pour boiling water over the cabbage and leave to cool for 30 minutes.
3. Remove the cabbage to leave liquid.
4. Pour the liquid into the small pots.
5. Add one food type to each pot.
6. Watch and see if the color changes

QUESTIONS TO THINK ABOUT

1. How did the color change with the different substances?
2. What color change happens with an acid?
3. What color change happens with a base?

FOR FURTHER RESEARCH

Research Anthocyanin to find out more about pH color changes that are taking place in your home-made indicator.

YOUR TURN

Imagine you are the editor of the Voice of Healing magazine. Collect together testimonies, photographs and teaching to make the first edition of the magazine. You can include testimonies from the God's Generals for Kids series, but also try to include testimonies some from your own life, members of your family, or from your church. You might also want to include some advertisements for Gospel meetings, like the original *Voice of Healing* magazine had. You can find samples of the magazine online

When you have finished your work, share it with your friends.

GET CREATIVE

Make a light picture.

1. Take a piece of black card and cut out a window shape from it, so the black card becomes the frame. You might want to cut out a church window, a cross or another shape.
2. Stick colored tissue paper to the back of the frame, covering over the holes.
3. Leave to dry.
4. Place the picture on a window and let the light shine through

To make it more creative, why not try using white card, draw a picture of a person and select which parts you want to shine the light through (perhaps parts of their face, or a design on their clothing). Cut out these parts and us the tissue paper as above

PHOTOS

William Branham

William Branham preparing to travel
and preach the Gospel

William Branham with a girl who had been healed

William Branham was a keen hunter

*Crowds press around William Branham
as he prays for the sick*

William Branham studying the Bible

AUTHORS' NOTE TO READERS AND PARENTS

Like William Branham, I believe that God can cure people miraculously today. However, I do *not* believe that this is the only way that God will work. God gives wisdom and knowledge to us to help us fight disease. Medical care can actually be part of God's plan for bringing relief and healing to His people. However, medicine still does not hold all the answers. I am in favor of both competent medical treatment and the power of prayer. I would not encourage anyone to neglect either of these at their time of need.

BIBLIOGRAPHY

Pearry Green, *William Branham: The Acts of a Prophet* (Tucson, AZ: Tucson Tabernacle 2011)

David Edwin Harrell Jr., *All Things are Possible: The Healing and Charismatic Revivals in Modern America* (Bloomington, IN: Indiana University Press 1978)

Owen Jorgensen, *Supernatural: The Life of William Branham Volumes I, II, III* (Coulee City, WA: Supernatural Christian Books 2011)

Roberts Liardon, *God's Generals: Why They Succeeded and Why Some Failed* (Tulsa, OK: Whitaker House 1996)

Gordon Lindsay, *William Branham: A Man Sent From God* (First published, 1950)

C. Douglas Weaver, *William Marrion Branham: The Healer Prophet* (Macon, GA: Mercer University Press 2000)

AUTHORS' CONTACT INFORMATION

ROBERTS LIARDON

Roberts Liardon Ministries, United States office:

P.O. Box 781888, Orlando, FL 32878

E-mail: Info1@robertsliardon.org

www.robertsliardon.org

United Kingdom/European office:

Roberts Liardon Ministries

22 Notting Hill Gate, Suite 125

London W11 3JE, UK

OLLY GOLDENBERG

BM Children Can, London WC1N 3XX, UK

info@childrencan.co.uk

www.childrencan.co.uk

 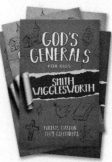

BEAUTY FROM ASHES
Donna Sparks

In a transparent and powerful manner, the author reveals how the Lord took her from the ashes of a life devastated by failed relationships and destructive behavior to bring her into a beautiful and powerful relationship with Him. The author encourages others to allow the Lord to do the same for them.

Donna Sparks is an Assemblies of God evangelist who travels widely to speak at women's conferences and retreats. She lives in Tennessee.

www.story-of-grace.com

www.facebook.com/
    donnasparksministries/

https://www.facebook.com/
    AuthorDonnaSparks/

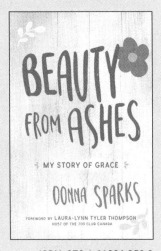

ISBN: 978-1-61036-252-8

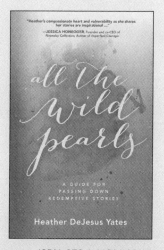

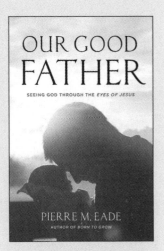